# Weather

**FIRST EDITION**
**Series Editor** Deborah Lock; **US Senior** Editor Shannon Beatty; **Art Director** Martin Wilson;
**Designer** Radhika Kapoor; **Managing Art Editor** Ahlawat Gunjan;
**Managing Editor** Soma Chowdhury; **DTP Designers** Anita Yadav, Vijay Khandwal;
**Picture Researcher** Nishwan Rasool; **Pre-Production Producer** Francesca Wardell;
**Jacket Designer** Martin Wilson; **Reading Consultant** Linda Gambrell, PhD

**THIS EDITION**
**Editorial Management** by Oriel Square
**Produced for DK** by WonderLab Group LLC
Jennifer Emmett, Erica Green, Kate Hale, *Founders*

**Editors** Grace Hill Smith, Libby Romero, Michaela Weglinski;
**Photography Editors** Kelley Miller, Annette Kiesow, Nicole DiMella;
**Managing Editor** Rachel Houghton; **Designers** Project Design Company; **Researcher** Michelle Harris;
**Copy Editor** Lori Merritt; **Indexer** Connie Binder; **Proofreader** Larry Shea;
**Reading Specialist** Dr. Jennifer Albro; **Curriculum Specialist** Elaine Larson

Published in the United States by DK Publishing
1745 Broadway, 20th Floor, New York, NY 10019

Copyright © 2023 Dorling Kindersley Limited
DK, a Division of Penguin Random House LLC
22 23 24 25 26 10 9 8 7 6 5 4 3 2 1
001–333456–May/2023

All rights reserved.
Without limiting the rights under the copyright reserved above, no part of this publication may be reproduced, stored in or introduced into a retrieval system, or transmitted, in any form, or by any means (electronic, mechanical, photocopying, recording, or otherwise), without the prior written permission of the copyright owner.
Published in Great Britain by Dorling Kindersley Limited

A catalog record for this book
is available from the Library of Congress.
HB ISBN: 978-0-7440-6794-1
PB ISBN: 978-0-7440-6795-8

DK books are available at special discounts when purchased in bulk for sales promotions, premiums,
fundraising, or educational use. For details, contact: DK Publishing Special Markets,
1745 Broadway, 20th Floor, New York, NY 10019
SpecialSales@dk.com

Printed and bound in China

The publisher would like to thank the following for their kind permission to reproduce their images:
a=above; c=center; b=below; l=left; r=right; t=top; b/g=background
**Dreamstime.com:** Sergey Galushko / Galdzer 4-5, Marsia16 13; **Shutterstock.com:** Jaromir Chalabala 14,
Jaren Jai Wicklund 26-17
Cover images: *Back:* **Shutterstock.com:** Sidachova Antonina bl

All other images © Dorling Kindersley
For more information see: www.dkimages.com

## For the curious
www.dk.com

Level 1

# Weather

Chris Jericho and Claire Oliver

# Contents

| **6**  | Look Outside! |
|--------|---------------|
| **8**  | Sun           |
| **10** | Clouds        |
| **12** | Fog           |
| **14** | Rain          |
| **18** | Storm         |
| **20** | Wind          |

| | |
|---|---|
| **22** | Gale |
| **24** | Snow |
| **28** | Rainbow |
| **30** | Glossary |
| **31** | Index |
| **32** | Quiz |

# Look Outside!
What's the weather like today?

cloudy

sunny

**rainy**

**snowy**

# Sun

Today is sunny and hot. The sun shines brightly.

## Clouds
Today is cloudy and warm.
The clouds can be fluffy or wispy.

fluffy

## Fog

Today is foggy and damp.
It is hard to see in the gray fog.

## Rain

Today is rainy and wet.
The rain pours down.

Pitter-patter!

raindrop

We splash in the puddles on rainy days. Splash!

boots

puddle

**Storm**

Tonight is stormy.
The lightning flashes,
and the thunder booms.

Crack!

# Wind

Today is windy and cold.
The wind blows the clothes.

# Gale
Today is very windy and very rainy.

The trees sway in the gale.

**Snow**

Today is snowy and freezing. The snow turns everything white.

**snowflake**

25

We wear warm clothes to play in the snow.

## Rainbow

Look!
The sun shines through the rain.
It makes a rainbow!
What will the weather be like tomorrow?

# Glossary

**gale**
a very strong and fast-moving wind

**lightning**
a flash of light in a storm

**puddle**
a small pool of water

**rainbow**
an arc of colors that forms when the sun shines through rain or mist

**snowflake**
a small, soft piece of frozen water (snow)

# Index

clouds   10
cloudy   6, 10
cold   20
damp   12
fog   12
foggy   12
freezing   24
gale   22, 23
hot   8
lightning   18, 19
puddle   16
rain   14, 28

rainbow   28
rainy   7, 14, 16, 22
snow   24, 26
snowflake   25
snowy   7, 24
stormy   18
sun   8, 28
sunny   6, 8
thunder   18
wet   14
wind   20
windy   20, 22

31

# Quiz

Answer the questions to see what you have learned. Check your answers with an adult.

1. What kind of weather makes it hard to see when you are outside?
2. What is the weather called when it is very windy and rainy?
3. What turns everything white outside?
4. When does a rainbow appear?
5. What do you like to do in your favorite kind of weather?

1. Fog  2. A gale  3. Snow
4. When the sun shines through the rain  5. Answers will vary